I0441970

.

This book Belongs to

_____

The Beauty of Random Things

"The Beauty of Random Things" was born of a desire to experiment with different art styles and mediums. Have you ever taken a walk through a forest or a garden and wondered at the way nature manages to make everything unique and individual? I began this book with that thought in mind. There is no specific theme to this book, the pictures came from various inspirations, but mostly I wanted to create a book filled with the type of images I, personally, would like to color.

I hope you enjoy your journey into the beauty of random things.

2016—Ionia Martin

This book is dedicated to my dad, the cowboy, who taught me how to look at the world and find beauty in negative spaces.

Color Test Page

Test your colors here

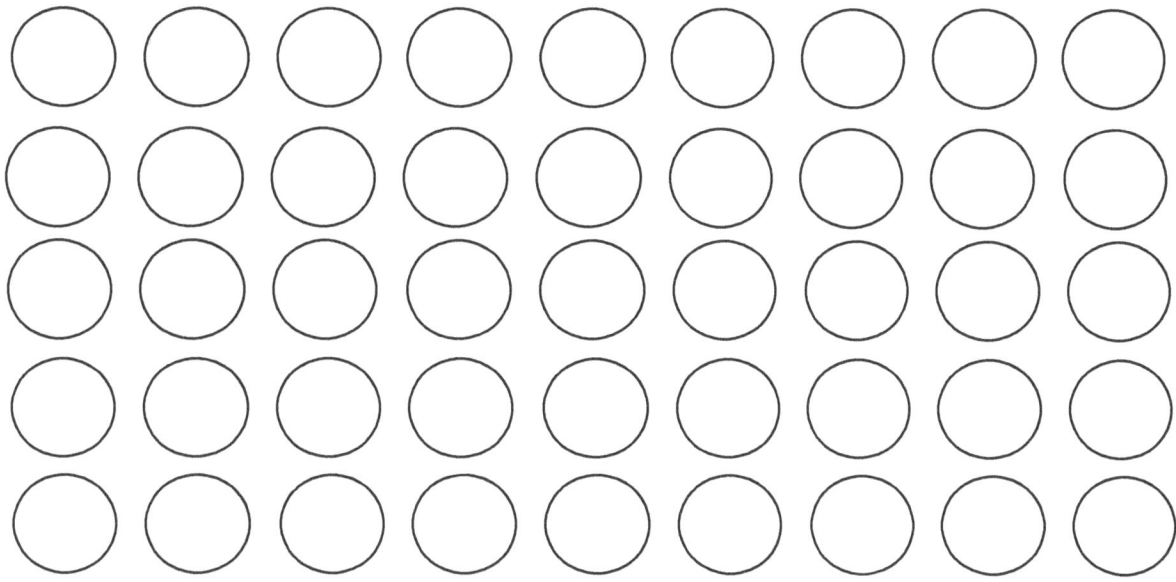

Cut out this page and insert behind the page you are currently coloring.

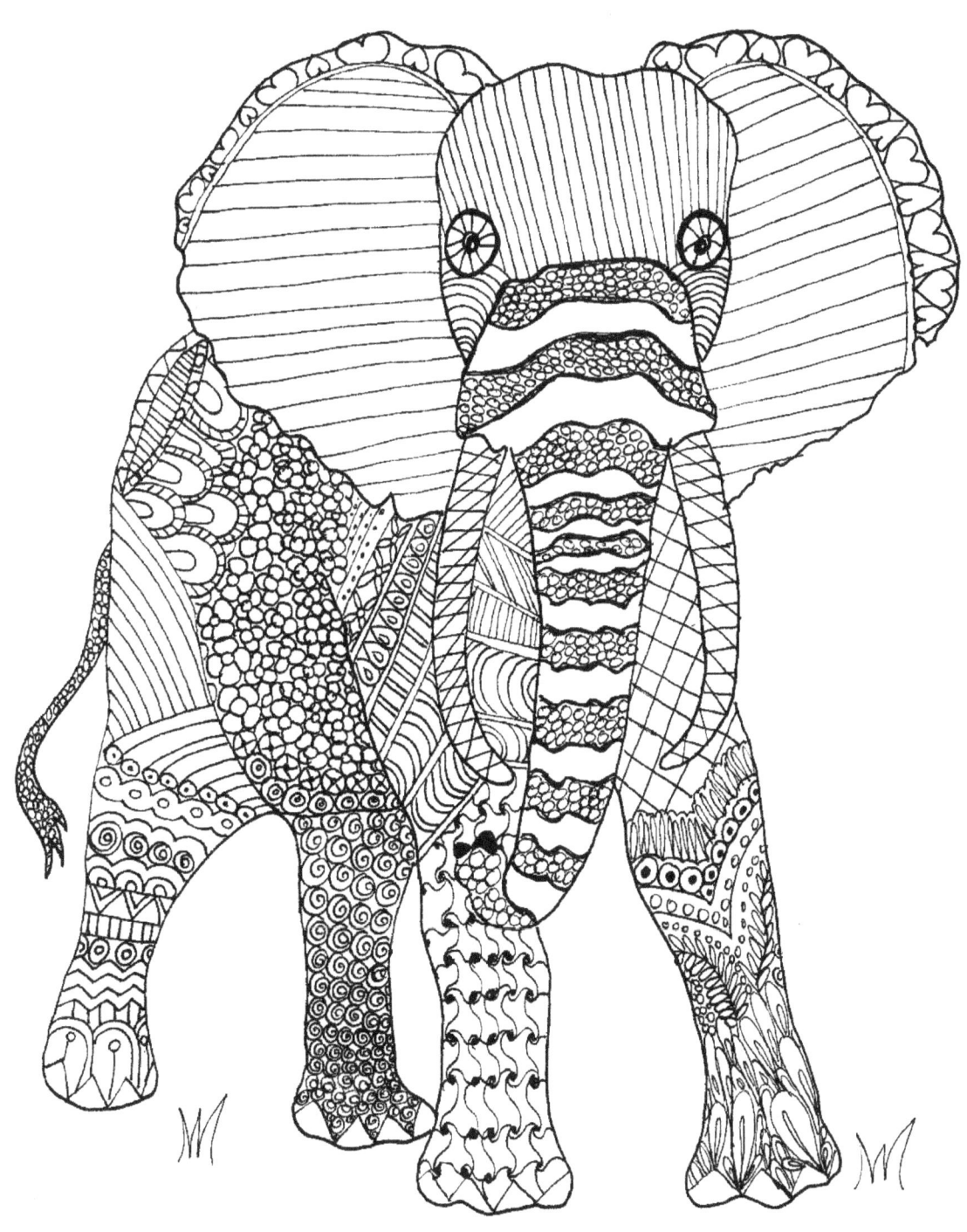

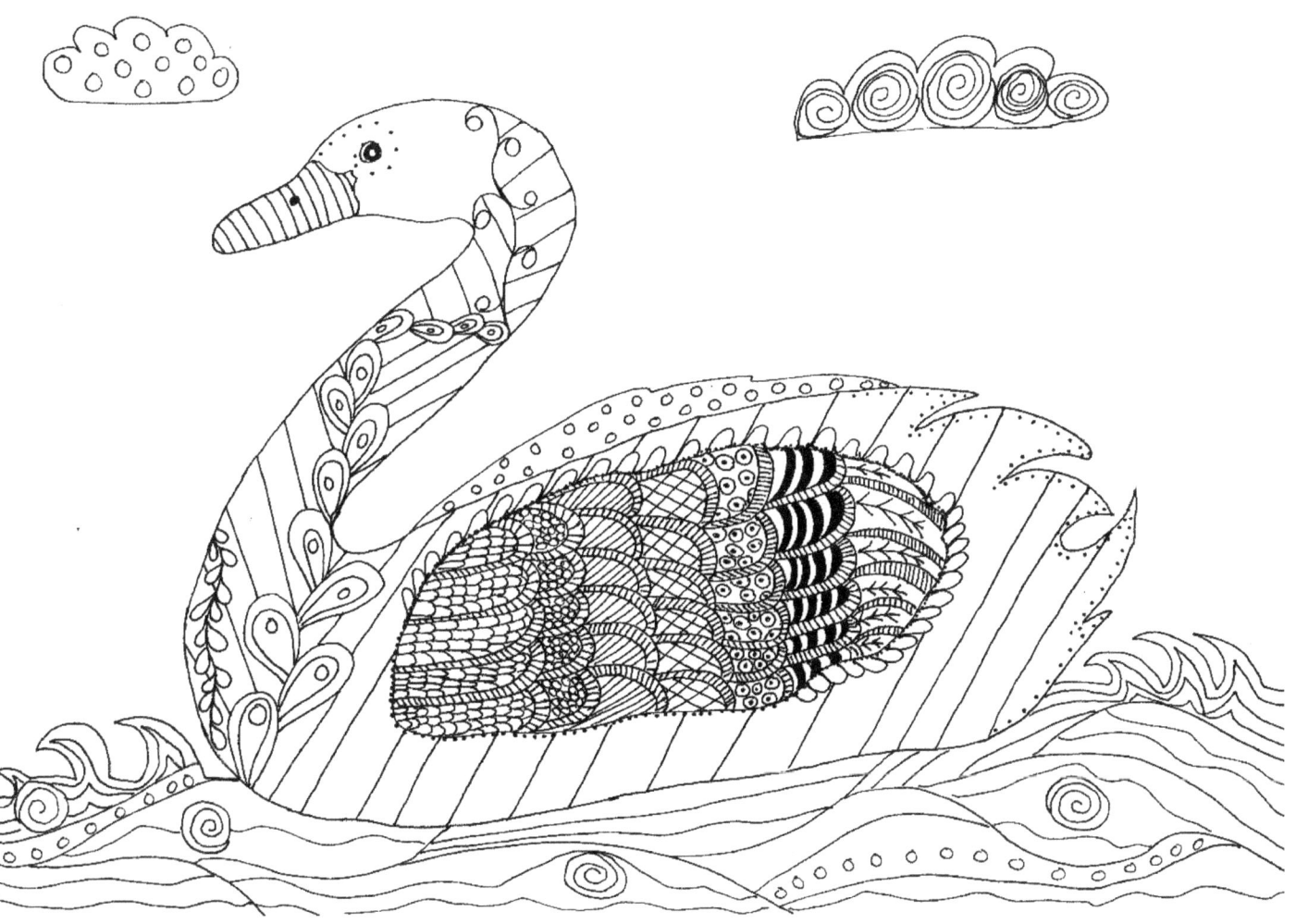

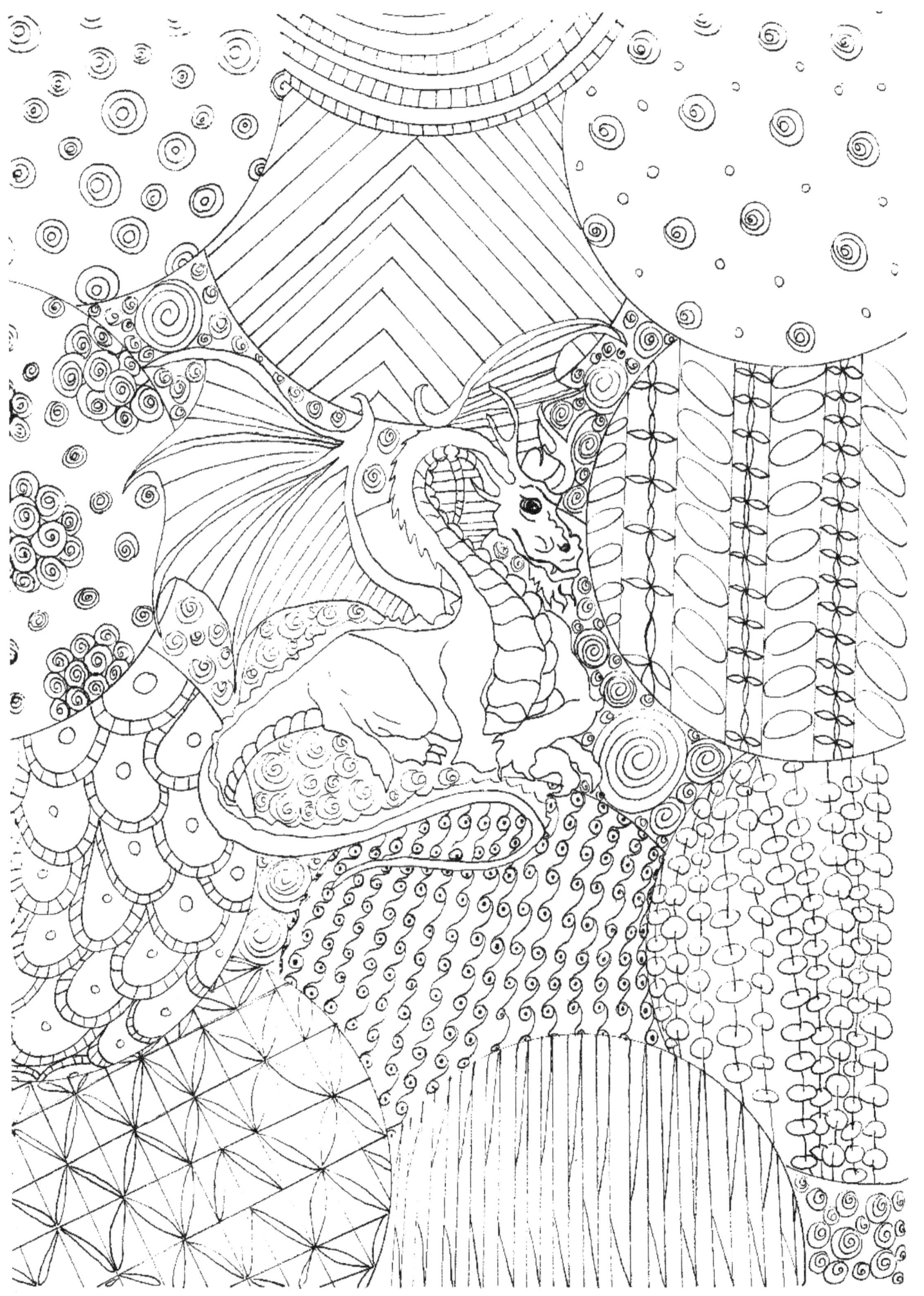